INDEX

	Page
Personal Record All my personal information	2
Funeral Arrangements Funeral preferences, Obituary, Personal instructions, Final deposition, Special wishes and instructions.	4
Genealogy / Family Use this space to record grandparents, siblings, spouse(s), children, step-children, grandchildren, etc	9
Financial Information Bank accounts & credit cards, Mortgage, Pension/Retirement plans, Insurance (health, car, homeowners, other), Location of important documents, Other important financial information.	13
Online Profiles Email, social media accounts, subscriptions or other important login information.	21
Notification Please be sure to notify these people of my passing.	27
Pets Information about my pets.	35
Belongings My belongings and what to do with them.	39
Special Thoughts Some thoughts I would like to share with my family and friends.	51
Notes Miscellaneous Information.	58

PERSONAL RECORD

First Name:	Middle name:
Last name:	
Address:	

City:	State:	Zip:
Phone number:		Years at address:
Place of birth:		Date of birth:

Seasonal residence:
Social Security Number:
Primary care physician :
Phone number:

Marital status:	☐ Single ☐ Married ☐ Divorced ☐ Widowed ☐ Living together
Maiden name:	
Spouse's name:	
Date and place of marriage:	

FATHER
First Name:
Father's birthplace:
MOTHER
First Name:
Mother's birthplace:

PERSONAL RECORD (Continued)

Education	
Highest grade completed: ☐ Elementary/Secondary ☐ College ☐ Other:	
College/university names:	Degree:

Career	
Occupation:	
Type of business/industry:	
Employer:	Phone:

Military	
Branch:	
Rank:	Serial number:
Location of discharge papers:	
Date and place of induction:	
Date and place of discharge:	

Notes:
_____
_____
_____
_____
_____
_____

FUNERAL ARRANGEMENTS

This page enables you and your family to know exactly which arrangements have been made and which ones remain to be determined.

INTERMENT RIGHTS

☐ Mausoleum	☐ Ground Burial
☐ Niche	☐ Cremation Garden
☐ Lawn Crypt	☐ Other

Date Selected

--------/--------/--------

_____

_____

OPENING AND CLOSING

Date Selected

--------/--------/--------

OUTER BURIAL CONTAINER

Date Selected

--------/--------/--------

FUNERAL/ MEMORIAL SERVICE

Date Selected

--------/--------/--------

MEMORIALIZATION

Date Selected

--------/--------/--------

TRANSPORTATION AND RELOCATION PROTECTION PLAN

Date Selected

--------/--------/--------

CASKET/URN

Date Selected

--------/--------/--------

PERSONAL PREFERENCE

☐ Flowers ☐ Readings ☐ Music

Date Selected

--------/--------/--------

_____

_____

_____

_____

FUNERAL ARRANGEMENTS (continued)

Funeral home to contact:	
Name:	
Counselor/Advisor:	
Address:	

FUNERAL PREFERENCES	
Place of service	
☐ Church	Name:
☐ Funeral Home	Name:
☐ Cemetery	Name:
☐ Other	Name:

Person to officiate:
Special Instructions:
Music selections:
Readings:

OBITUARY
Name of newspaper(s):
Name of website(s):
Other:
Visitation: ☐ Yes ☐ No ☐ Public ☐ Private
Casket: ☐ Open ☐ Closed

FUNERAL ARRANGEMENTS (continued)

FINAL DEPOSITION
☐ Earth burial ☐ Mausoleum entombment ☐ Cremation/inurnment
☐ Other (please specify)
NAME OF CEMETERY/MAUSOLEUM
Address
Phone:
Description of burial property:
Casket selection:
URN SELECTION
Vault selection:
Personalization choices:
PERMANENT MEMORIAL
Type:
Inscription:
Flowers:
Personal touches/items to display:
Special services/ceremonies (fraternal, military, spiritual, etc.)

FUNERAL ARRANGEMENTS (continued)

Personal Instruction	
Clothing:	☐ Stays on ☐ Return to family
Glasses:	☐ Stays on ☐ Return to family
Jewelry:	☐ Stays on ☐ Return to family
Other:	☐ Stays on ☐ Return to family
Other:	☐ Stays on ☐ Return to family
Other:	☐ Stays on ☐ Return to family

Religious items:

Suggested memorial contributions:

Pallbearers:

FUNERAL ARRANGEMENTS (continued)

Other requests:
_____
_____
_____
_____
_____
_____
_____
_____
_____
_____

Special notes regarding personal memorial:
_____
_____
_____
_____
_____
_____
_____
_____
_____
_____

Genealogy/Family

Use this space to record grandparents, siblings, spouse(s), children, step-children, grandchildren, etc

Genealogy/Family 1

Use this space to record grandparents, siblings, spouse(s), children, step-children, grandchildren, etc

Name:

Name:

Name:

Name:

Name:

Name:

Name:

Name:

Name:

Name:

Genealogy/Family 2

Use this space to record grandparents, siblings, spouse(s), children, step-children, grandchildren, etc

Name:

Name:

Name:

Name:

Name:

Name:

Name:

Name:

Name:

Name:

Genealogy/Family 3

Use this space to record grandparents, siblings, spouse(s), children, step-children, grandchildren, etc

Name:

Name:

Name:

Name:

Name:

Name:

Name:

Name:

Name:

Name:

Financial Information

Financial Information 1

BANKING

Bank Name/branch:
Type of account ☐ Checking ☐ Savings
Username:
Password:

Bank Name/branch:
Type of account ☐ Checking ☐ Savings
Username:
Password:

Bank Name/branch:
Type of account ☐ Checking ☐ Savings
Username:
Password:

Bank Name/branch:
Type of account ☐ Checking ☐ Savings
Username:
Password:

Financial Information 2

CREDIT CARDS

☐ Visa ☐ Mastercard ☐ American Express ☐ Other:	
Account number:	Exp. Date:
Username:	
Password:	

☐ Visa ☐ Mastercard ☐ American Express ☐ Other:	
Account number:	Exp. Date:
Username:	
Password:	

☐ Visa ☐ Mastercard ☐ American Express ☐ Other:	
Account number:	Exp. Date:
Username:	
Password:	

☐ Visa ☐ Mastercard ☐ American Express ☐ Other:	
Account number:	Exp. Date:
Username:	
Password:	

Financial Information 3

MORTGAGE
Lender
Account number:
Phone number
Location:

PENSION/RETIREMENT PLANS
Company name
Account number:
Phone number:
Location:
Company name
Account number:
Phone number:
Location:
Company name
Account number:
Phone number:
Location:

Financial Information 4

PENSION/RETIREMENT PLANS (CONTINUED)
Company name:
Account number:
Phone number
Location:
Company name:
Account number:
Phone number:
Location:
Company name:
Account number:
Phone number:
Location:
Company name:
Account number:
Phone number:
Location:

Financial Information 5

INSURANCE (HOMEOWNERS, HEALTH, CAR, OTHER)	
Company:	Agent:
Phone number:	
Policy number:	
Beneficiary:	
Company:	Agent:
Phone number:	
Policy number:	
Beneficiary:	
Company:	Agent:
Phone number:	
Policy number:	
Beneficiary:	
Company:	Agent:
Phone number:	
Policy number:	
Beneficiary:	

Financial Information 6

LOCATION OF IMPORTANT DOCUMENTS
Safe deposit box location:
Box number:
Keys location:
Birth Certificate:
Children's birth certificate(s):
Last will and testament:
Funeral and cemetery arrangement documents:
Real estate deeds:
Income tax records:
Car registration/title:
Other documents:

Financial Information 7
Other financial information and instructions

Online Profiles

Email, social media accounts, subscriptions or other important login information.

Online Profiles 1

List your email, social media accounts or other important login information

Account name:
Web address/URL:
Username:
Password:
☐ Keep account open ☐ Close this account
Other Information:

Account name:
Web address/URL:
Username:
Password:
☐ Keep account open ☐ Close this account
Other Information:

Account name:
Web address/URL:
Username:
Password:
☐ Keep account open ☐ Close this account
Other Information:

Online Profiles 2
List your email, social media accounts or other important login information

Account name:
Web address/URL:
Username:
Password:
☐ Keep account open ☐ Close this account
Other Information:

Account name:
Web address/URL:
Username:
Password:
☐ Keep account open ☐ Close this account
Other Information:

Account name:
Web address/URL:
Username:
Password:
☐ Keep account open ☐ Close this account
Other Information:

Online Profiles 3
List your email, social media accounts or other important login information

Account name:
Web address/URL:
Username:
Password:
☐ Keep account open ☐ Close this account
Other Information:

Account name:
Web address/URL:
Username:
Password:
☐ Keep account open ☐ Close this account
Other Information:

Account name:
Web address/URL:
Username:
Password:
☐ Keep account open ☐ Close this account
Other Information:

Online Profiles 4
List your email, social media accounts or other important login information

Account name:
Web address/URL:
Username:
Password:
☐ Keep account open ☐ Close this account
Other Information:

Account name:
Web address/URL:
Username:
Password:
☐ Keep account open ☐ Close this account
Other Information:

Account name:
Web address/URL:
Username:
Password:
☐ Keep account open ☐ Close this account
Other Information:

Online Profiles 5
List your email, social media accounts or other important login information

Account name:
Web address/URL:
Username:
Password:
☐ Keep account open ☐ Close this account
Other Information:

Account name:
Web address/URL:
Username:
Password:
☐ Keep account open ☐ Close this account
Other Information:

Account name:
Web address/URL:
Username:
Password:
☐ Keep account open ☐ Close this account
Other Information:

Notifications

Please be sure to notify these people of my passing

NOTIFICATION
Please be sure to notify these people of my passing:

Name:
Relationship:
Address:
Phone:
Email:
Other Information/ special message:

Name:
Relationship:
Address:
Phone:
Email:
Other Information/ special message:

Name:
Relationship:
Address:
Phone:
Email:
Other information/special message:

NOTIFICATION
Please be sure to notify these people of my passing:

Name:
Relationship:
Address:
Phone:
Email:
Other Information/ special message:

Name:
Relationship:
Address:
Phone:
Email:
Other Information/ special message:

Name:
Relationship:
Address:
Phone:
Email:
Other information/special message:

NOTIFICATION
Please be sure to notify these people of my passing:

Name:
Relationship:
Address:
Phone:
Email:
Other Information/ special message:

Name:
Relationship:
Address:
Phone:
Email:
Other Information/ special message:

Name:
Relationship:
Address:
Phone:
Email:
Other information/special message:

NOTIFICATION
Please be sure to notify these people of my passing:

Name:
Relationship:
Address:
Phone:
Email:
Other Information/ special message:

Name:
Relationship:
Address:
Phone:
Email:
Other Information/ special message:

Name:
Relationship:
Address:
Phone:
Email:
Other information/special message:

NOTIFICATION
Please be sure to notify these people of my passing:

Name:
Relationship:
Address:
Phone:
Email:
Other Information/ special message:

Name:
Relationship:
Address:
Phone:
Email:
Other Information/ special message:

Name:
Relationship:
Address:
Phone:
Email:
Other information/special message:

NOTIFICATION
Please be sure to notify these people of my passing:

Name:
Relationship:
Address:
Phone:
Email:
Other Information/ special message:

Name:
Relationship:
Address:
Phone:
Email:
Other Information/ special message:

Name:
Relationship:
Address:
Phone:
Email:
Other information/special message:

NOTIFICATION
Please be sure to notify these people of my passing:

Name:
Relationship:
Address:
Phone:
Email:
Other Information/ special message:

Name:
Relationship:
Address:
Phone:
Email:
Other Information/ special message:

Name:
Relationship:
Address:
Phone:
Email:
Other information/special message:

Pets

PETS
Information about my pets

Name:	
Kind of animal:	Age:
License or ID information:	
Who will take care of him/her:	
Name:	Telephone:
Other Information (health, diet, insurance etc.)	

Name:	
Kind of animal:	Age:
License or ID information:	
Who will take care of him/her:	
Name:	Telephone:
Other Information (health, diet, insurance etc.)	

Name:	
Kind of animal:	Age:
License or ID information:	
Who will take care of him/her:	
Name:	Telephone:
Other Information (health, diet, insurance etc.)	

PETS
Information about my pets

Name:		
Kind of animal:		Age:
License or ID information:		
Who will take care of him/her:		
Name:	Telephone:	
Other Information (health, diet, insurance etc.)		

Name:		
Kind of animal:		Age:
License or ID information:		
Who will take care of him/her:		
Name:	Telephone:	
Other Information (health, diet, insurance etc.)		

Name:		
Kind of animal:		Age:
License or ID information:		
Who will take care of him/her:		
Name:	Telephone:	
Other Information (health, diet, insurance etc.)		

PETS (continued)
Information about my pets

Name:		
Kind of animal:		Age:
License or ID information:		
Who will take care of him/her:		
Name:	Telephone:	
Other Information (health, diet, insurance etc.)		

Name:		
Kind of animal:		Age:
License or ID information:		
Who will take care of him/her:		
Name:	Telephone:	
Other Information (health, diet, insurance etc.)		

Notes:
_____
_____
_____
_____
_____
_____

Belongings

And what to do with them

BELONGINGS
And what to do with them

Item:	
Location:	
☐ Give to	Name:
☐ Give to charity	Name:
☐ Other	Describe:
More Information:	

Item:	
Location:	
☐ Give to :	Name:
☐ Give to charity	Name:
☐ Other	Describe:
More Information:	

Item:	
Location:	
☐ Give to :	Name:
☐ Give to charity	Name:
☐ Other	Describe:
More Information:	

BELONGINGS
And what to do with them

Item:	
Location:	
☐ Give to	Name:
☐ Give to charity	Name:
☐ Other	Describe:
More Information:	

Item:	
Location:	
☐ Give to :	Name:
☐ Give to charity	Name:
☐ Other	Describe:
More Information:	

Item:	
Location:	
☐ Give to :	Name:
☐ Give to charity	Name:
☐ Other	Describe:
More Information:	

BELONGINGS
And what to do with them

Item:	
Location:	
☐ Give to	Name:
☐ Give to charity	Name:
☐ Other	Describe:
More Information:	

Item:	
Location:	
☐ Give to :	Name:
☐ Give to charity	Name:
☐ Other	Describe:
More Information:	

Item:	
Location:	
☐ Give to :	Name:
☐ Give to charity	Name:
☐ Other	Describe:
More Information:	

BELONGINGS
And what to do with them

Item:	
Location:	
☐ Give to	Name:
☐ Give to charity	Name:
☐ Other	Describe:
More Information:	

Item:	
Location:	
☐ Give to :	Name:
☐ Give to charity	Name:
☐ Other	Describe:
More Information:	

Item:	
Location:	
☐ Give to :	Name:
☐ Give to charity	Name:
☐ Other	Describe:
More Information:	

BELONGINGS
And what to do with them

Item:	
Location:	
☐ Give to	Name:
☐ Give to charity	Name:
☐ Other	Describe:
More Information:	

Item:	
Location:	
☐ Give to :	Name:
☐ Give to charity	Name:
☐ Other	Describe:
More Information:	

Item:	
Location:	
☐ Give to :	Name:
☐ Give to charity	Name:
☐ Other	Describe:
More Information:	

BELONGINGS
And what to do with them

Item:	
Location:	
☐ Give to	Name:
☐ Give to charity	Name:
☐ Other	Describe:
More Information:	

Item:	
Location:	
☐ Give to :	Name:
☐ Give to charity	Name:
☐ Other	Describe:
More Information:	

Item:	
Location:	
☐ Give to :	Name:
☐ Give to charity	Name:
☐ Other	Describe:
More Information:	

BELONGINGS
And what to do with them

Item:	
Location:	
☐ Give to	Name:
☐ Give to charity	Name:
☐ Other	Describe:
More Information:	

Item:	
Location:	
☐ Give to :	Name:
☐ Give to charity	Name:
☐ Other	Describe:
More Information:	

Item:	
Location:	
☐ Give to :	Name:
☐ Give to charity	Name:
☐ Other	Describe:
More Information:	

BELONGINGS
And what to do with them

Item:	
Location:	
☐ Give to	Name:
☐ Give to charity	Name:
☐ Other	Describe:
More Information:	

Item:	
Location:	
☐ Give to :	Name:
☐ Give to charity	Name:
☐ Other	Describe:
More Information:	

Item:	
Location:	
☐ Give to :	Name:
☐ Give to charity	Name:
☐ Other	Describe:
More Information:	

BELONGINGS
And what to do with them

Item:	
Location:	
☐ Give to	Name:
☐ Give to charity	Name:
☐ Other	Describe:
More Information:	

Item:	
Location:	
☐ Give to :	Name:
☐ Give to charity	Name:
☐ Other	Describe:
More Information:	

Item:	
Location:	
☐ Give to :	Name:
☐ Give to charity	Name:
☐ Other	Describe:
More Information:	

BELONGINGS
And what to do with them

Item:	
Location:	
☐ Give to	Name:
☐ Give to charity	Name:
☐ Other	Describe:
More Information:	

Item:	
Location:	
☐ Give to :	Name:
☐ Give to charity	Name:
☐ Other	Describe:
More Information:	

Item:	
Location:	
☐ Give to :	Name:
☐ Give to charity	Name:
☐ Other	Describe:
More Information:	

BELONGINGS
And what to do with them

Item:	
Location:	
☐ Give to	Name:
☐ Give to charity	Name:
☐ Other	Describe:
More Information:	

Item:	
Location:	
☐ Give to :	Name:
☐ Give to charity	Name:
☐ Other	Describe:
More Information:	

Item:	
Location:	
☐ Give to :	Name:
☐ Give to charity	Name:
☐ Other	Describe:
More Information:	

Special Thoughts...

SPECIAL THOUGHTS I WOULD LIKE TO SHARE WITH MY FAMILY AND FRIENDS

_____
_____
_____
_____
_____
_____
_____
_____
_____
_____
_____
_____
_____
_____
_____
_____
_____
_____
_____
_____
_____
_____
_____

SPECIAL THOUGHTS I WOULD LIKE TO SHARE WITH MY FAMILY AND FRIENDS (continued)

_____
_____
_____
_____
_____
_____
_____
_____
_____
_____
_____
_____
_____
_____
_____
_____
_____
_____
_____
_____
_____
_____
_____
_____

SPECIAL THOUGHTS I WOULD LIKE TO SHARE WITH MY FAMILY AND FRIENDS (continued)

SPECIAL THOUGHTS I WOULD LIKE TO SHARE WITH MY FAMILY AND FRIENDS (continued)

SPECIAL THOUGHTS I WOULD LIKE TO SHARE WITH MY FAMILY AND FRIENDS (continued)

_____
_____
_____
_____
_____
_____
_____
_____
_____
_____
_____
_____
_____
_____
_____
_____
_____
_____
_____
_____
_____
_____
_____
_____
_____

SPECIAL THOUGHTS I WOULD LIKE TO SHARE WITH MY FAMILY AND FRIENDS (continued)

Notes

Notes

Notes

www.ingramcontent.com/pod-product-compliance
Lightning Source LLC
Chambersburg PA
CBHW050310220526
45465CB00005B/1929